I Am

Escape Distractions, Unlock Your Imagination & Unleash Your Potential

Bruce Kasanoff and Amy Blaschka

Published by
Intuitive Leaps Media
Park City, UT 84060
ISBN 978-1-941115-04-6

For reprint information and other inquiries, please visit
IntuitiveLeaps.net.

The cover image entitled "Imagine This" is a photograph by
Bruce Kasanoff. To learn more about his images, please visit
Kasanoff.com/art.

Contents

Please join us at I-Am-Books.com
to exchange experiences, insights,
and observations sparked by this book.

Introduction

An antidote for a distracted, multitasking world...

If you're reading this, chances are you're in between tasks or meetings. Or errands. Or adding things to your to-do list. Or a million other things that occupy your mind all at once.

And now for the good news: right at this moment, you are actively considering another path. You're thinking about taking a little time each day for yourself, away from life's craziness, to just... be.

We get it because we've been there, too.

But then we started considering ways to escape the distractions and obligations that are so prevalent in today's multitasking world. In fact, you may not even realize it, but a fog of these thoughts, distractions, obligations, and beliefs surround you.

This is not only true for you, but it is also true for each of us. It's part of the human condition. Your perceptions are shaped by your parents, relatives, friends, culture, health, income level, race, nationality, and environment.

This is neither a good nor bad thing. It is simply a reality.

What if, we thought, *each of us regularly took a few minutes to break free from all of the thoughts, interruptions, duties, and beliefs competing for our attention?*

(By the way, "each of us" includes YOU.)

That would be great! In these moments, the fog lifts, swirls, changes. Reality shifts. Rules disintegrate. Possibilities emerge.

These moments are precious, a gift from beyond the edges of your day-to-day awareness. They are never to be taken for granted.

You may consider, perhaps for the first time, the infinite array of answers to complete this simple yet complex phrase: "I am... ."

So we created the short meditations in this slim book to help unleash your creativity, imagination, and potential.

We acknowledge that for some, just the mention of the word meditation causes discomfort. "I'm not one of those people," you might say. Or, "I've never meditated before and wouldn't know how to start."

But the fact that you're still reading this tells us that you think it might be time to try. And we're here to help you get going.

In our experience, when you slow down, step back, and quiet your mind, you consider different possibilities and make room for new ideas. Innovative solutions. Intuitive leaps.

And it's those creative insights that might never see the light of day were it not for you intentionally creating time and space for them to appear.

"So, Bruce and Amy," you might be saying, "this sounds intriguing, but how can I get into that zone?"

We're glad you asked.

Since we're all busy, we knew it had to be something relatively quick. And it had to be easy, with no special equipment required. (Except this little gem of a book, of course.)

We suggest you read one—yes, just one—of the passages, then close your eyes and merely focus on the entry you've just read. Take five minutes for yourself. (Or 10. Or 20. It's up to you.)

That's it. Simple, right?

As you reflect on the passage and allow yourself to be drawn inward, you may find that you're rewarded with new ideas and thinking. You may consider possibilities and see connections where none seemed to exist before.

The meditations we offer here serve as a catalyst to relax your mind and unleash your imagination. To make that clear, we have left every other page blank, so that you may capture any ideas and observations you conceive. You might consider making a note of each meditation you do and then describe your experiences. If you're one of those people who doesn't like to write in books, you can attach a sticky note in that space. This is also why we have resisted the temptation to offer a digital version of this book.

One more thing: this book is YOUR resource. Feel free to use it as you wish, whether that means going through each entry in order, or just flipping to a random page. The beauty of a book like this lies in its ability to adapt to its owner's wants and needs.

We hope that you will come to look forward to this practice… to cherish those reflections that will surprise, delight, stun, and awaken you. And in doing so, you will unleash your creativity, imagination, and potential.

Enjoy your moments.

Bruce and Amy
January 2018

Use this space to capture your thoughts, ideas, and sketches… or simply to note when you reflect on a passage.

I am... perceptive

Non-obvious solutions appear to me, seemingly without any effort on my part.

Subtle changes that others may miss, I tend to see.

When the world shifts, even in small ways, it often catches my attention.

This is not because I am smarter or better than others. It is because I am willing to be open and aware. I am willing to suspend judgment, observe without labeling, and step away— at least for a short period— from what I believe to be true.

Right now I take time simply to be perceptive, open, and aware.

Use this space to capture your thoughts, ideas, and sketches...
or simply to note when you reflect on a passage.

I am... an ocean

Deep and wide and blue. Breathtaking.

A dichotomy of calm and wild forces. My power is responsive. Cyclical. Rhythmic as it shifts with the tides of life.

I breathe in the warmth of the blazing sun and exhale a salty mist of cooling spray.

I extend to all corners of the Earth, from rocky shorelines and sandy coves to glacial drifts and emerald marshes.

I have the potential to sustain life, to provide beauty, to calm and to nourish, to transport people to faraway places and magical experiences.

And I willingly invite others to immerse themselves in my depths and emerge renewed by my healing waters.

*Use this space to capture your thoughts, ideas, and sketches...
or simply to note when you reflect on a passage.*

I am... silence

A quiet so profound, it absorbs and mutes everything that dares challenge it. Like a blanket of snow unfathomably deep. Spend time with me, and you will start to question the very existence of sound. I not only banish noise from my presence but also erase its very existence.

(   )

Use this space to capture your thoughts, ideas, and sketches... or simply to note when you reflect on a passage.

I am... a whisper in the wind, barely audible

Can you hear me? If you're not careful, you'll miss my message as you rush about multi-tasking, and busy yourself being busy.

Slow down.

Remove all distractions.

Exhale.

Are you listening? The answers are all around you; you just need to be receptive to receiving them.

Quiet your mind and open yourself up to the wisdom of the Universe.

Use this space to capture your thoughts, ideas, and sketches... or simply to note when you reflect on a passage.

I am... a single candle in the darkness

My heart is filled with joy. I dance in the darkness, playful and invigorated. As I burn, wisps of smoke rise from the tip of my flame, spreading the magical scent of possibility, hope, and goodwill. Just as I do, my smoke dances and twists; it rises higher and higher and higher still.

The darkness around me stretches forever, but that only makes my light more important. I can be seen across vast distances, and my light will burn forever and ever more.

Use this space to capture your thoughts, ideas, and sketches... or simply to note when you reflect on a passage.

I am... magnetic

Others are pulled into my orbit, lured by my inner light, which glows bright and strong and true.

My ability to attract goodness is powerful, and its intensity grows as my focus does.

I am a force field of hope, an aura of encouragement, a beacon of positivity. I am a generator of pure love whose spirit can influence anyone in its presence.

I captivate and engage.

I am irresistible.

Use this space to capture your thoughts, ideas, and sketches... or simply to note when you reflect on a passage.

I am... not my body

This is a truth that was long hidden. Day after day, year after year, I experienced the world through my body, and it was so easy to perceive that:

I = flesh and blood

Untrue. I existed long before this body and will survive eons after it has disintegrated. Using words to describe me is senseless; words are what this body needs to communicate, but this body cannot grasp what I really am.

Only by letting this body rest for a few minutes can I sense my own existence.

Too many words already. It's time to stop... and... just... be... me.

Use this space to capture your thoughts, ideas, and sketches... or simply to note when you reflect on a passage.

I am... a blank canvas

Open to infinite possibilities.

Willing to embrace change and adventure.

Ready to fill my frame with color and movement and texture and pattern.

To live fully, to feel deeply, and to experience all that life has to offer.

*Use this space to capture your thoughts, ideas, and sketches…
or simply to note when you reflect on a passage.*

I am... complicated

Happy.

Frustrated.

Loving. Envious.

Depressed.

Compassion. Confident.

A confidante. A bit of a gossip.

Playful. Sullen. Withdrawn.

In denial.

Getting better.

Reaching higher.

Uncertain.

Alone. Along. Amazing. Ambitious.

Or maybe not.

*Use this space to capture your thoughts, ideas, and sketches...
or simply to note when you reflect on a passage.*

I am... a singular snowflake

Floating through the silent Aspens
Caught on an outstretched tongue

Use this space to capture your thoughts, ideas, and sketches... or simply to note when you reflect on a passage.

I am... so tiny

You can't see me.
You can't hear me.
Take the smallest thing you can imagine, and divide it by one million. I am smaller than that.

I am such a tiny speck that time does not exist in my life. There is no past, present, or future.
I am smaller than everything.

*Use this space to capture your thoughts, ideas, and sketches...
or simply to note when you reflect on a passage.*

I am... a chameleon

Able to effortlessly adapt to my surroundings.

I shape-shift, taking on many forms and personas and roles.

Hidden in plain sight, yet always observing the world and its happenings.

Ever present (even if you can't see   ).

Use this space to capture your thoughts, ideas, and sketches...
or simply to note when you reflect on a passage.

I am... giving myself permission...

...to try

...to stumble

...to fail (many times)

...to fall short of my own high expectations

...to confront my weaknesses

...to admit I am human

...to learn from my mistakes

...to not have all the answers

...to acknowledge my strengths

...to be kind, even when it's hard to do so

...to not worry about what others think

...to let go of elements of my life that aren't working

...to be unapologetically me (and to be okay with that)

...and maybe, to succeed.

*Use this space to capture your thoughts, ideas, and sketches...
or simply to note when you reflect on a passage.*

I am... intuitive

Answers come to me from sources I do not understand, but that does not lessen their value. I know that most humans underestimate the degree to which each of our brains is an intuition machine. We use intuition to recognize colors and shapes, to distinguish danger from safety, and to recognize friend or foe.

Even beyond that, I embrace my intuitive side because time and time again it has brought me gifts of knowledge, insight, and opportunity. My intuition is more than mere "gut feel." It is the highest form of intelligence.

I close my eyes now to better pay attention to this treasured side of me.

Use this space to capture your thoughts, ideas, and sketches... or simply to note when you reflect on a passage.

I am... courageous

I try new things, even if I'm not ready.

I allow myself to be vulnerable, for that's where growth takes place.

I embrace new beginnings, as they are the gateway to life's adventures and my fulfillment.

I take risks, not to be foolhardy but to explore the possibilities of what might be.

Instead of hiding in the shadows, I step in the light. And by doing so, I encourage others to do the same.

Use this space to capture your thoughts, ideas, and sketches... or simply to note when you reflect on a passage.

I am... kind, engaged, and thoughtful

To be kind is to show consideration and compassion for others. It also demonstrates I have the ability to make a difference.

To be engaged is to participate in the world, to give my all to each undertaking. And, yes, to make a difference.

Being thoughtful shows I am capable of insight, empathy, and—most importantly—to rise above my emotions and instincts to do what is right.

It gives me enormous satisfaction to be all three, and so I take the time to reflect on how to spend even more time at the intersection of these three qualities:

Kind, engaged, and thoughtful.

Use this space to capture your thoughts, ideas, and sketches...
or simply to note when you reflect on a passage.

I am... on fire!

That's how I'll answer the question if you ask me how I am.

But you probably won't even need to ask because it will be apparent the instant I enter a room: the undeniable scent of confidence.

Not to be confused with its evil twin, cockiness, my confidence is evidenced by the quiet assuredness of someone completely comfortable in his or her own skin.

There is no need for me to compare myself to and compete with others.

In fact, I'm able to use this trait to put people at ease and break down barriers for more meaningful and deeper connections.

And the good news is that my inner fire is always there, ready to burn brighter than any uncertainty or doubt ever could.

Use this space to capture your thoughts, ideas, and sketches… or simply to note when you reflect on a passage.

I am... gently wishing

The trick to getting what I want is not to want it too much but still want it enough.

The art of gentle wishing takes practice. It means visualizing in your mind what you want, then letting it go. Wanting too much or too obsessively won't work. Wanting it without visualizing it won't work. This sounded odd when I first heard of it, but for some reason, gentle wishing really works.

I can wish for a parking space on a crowded day or for my down-on-her-luck friend to finally get the job she needs. I can make a gentle wish for almost anything.

So now I close my eyes and make this gentle wish...

Use this space to capture your thoughts, ideas, and sketches... or simply to note when you reflect on a passage.

I am... unexpected good news

I am that feeling when, out of the blue, you get news that fills your heart with joy.

A completely unexpected message of goodness that washes over you like a wave of happiness, with the power to instantly uplift and improve your mood.

And the best part about my surprise? Those good vibes tend to multiply and spread cheer, thereby creating a virtuous cycle.

*Use this space to capture your thoughts, ideas, and sketches...
or simply to note when you reflect on a passage.*

I am... selfish

I'm compassionate and kind. Maybe even considerate. But I'm also selfish... and this is a good thing.

I'm selfish enough to need the people around me to do well, for if they suffer, the quality of my life will suffer, too.

I'm selfish enough to insist that the people in my community have access to education and healthcare, for if they lack either then I will not be happy with the coming years.

I'm selfish enough to fight for equality and respect because I simply don't wish to live in a world that lacks either.

And now I take a few moments to contemplate other ways that my selfishness may make the world a better place.

*Use this space to capture your thoughts, ideas, and sketches…
or simply to note when you reflect on a passage.*

I am... you

When I take a moment to get out of my own head, to observe
the world from another point of view, amazing things happen.

I gain clarity.
Perspective.

One step removed from myself and walking in your shoes, I find
more empathy and compassion.

I share your hopes, your fears, and your dreams.
I am awed by my newfound ability to meld into you. To become
you. I am transformed.

We are connected.
We are the same.
We are one.

Use this space to capture your thoughts, ideas, and sketches... or simply to note when you reflect on a passage.

I am... ever better

There are no limits to my growth. Just because I could not do something yesterday does not mean I cannot do it at some point in the future.

What I can learn, who I can meet, what I can achieve... these are limited only by a (false) belief that these things are limited.

Every time I close my eyes and unlock my imagination, I open the doors to becoming ever better, to growing without limits, and to becoming a better version of myself.

This is my wish and my recognition: I have no limits.

Use this space to capture your thoughts, ideas, and sketches… or simply to note when you reflect on a passage.

I am... an oak tree

Formed slowly, but steadily over decades, each year bringing more substance and growth.

My beauty lies in my gnarled imperfection, my web of twisting branches and experiences.

I'm resilient, steadfast and strong, yet flexible enough to sway and bend with life's storms and to resist the fires that attempt to destroy me.

It takes a lot to bring me down.

I will protect you, fuel you, support you. I will always stand by you, a silent sentry guarding your path.

Use this space to capture your thoughts, ideas, and sketches...
or simply to note when you reflect on a passage.

I am... wandering

So much of my time is spent heading towards something, but right now I am doing the opposite. I take a step in one direction, then three in another. I'm not limited by gravity or physics or time.

Sometimes I go up, then down. I float gently, then accelerate beyond the speed of light. Colors come and go, shifting and blending together. One moment I am moving, another resting. Nothing compels me, although I am curious about what will happen next.

Never before have I been this relaxed and open. I'm wandering, exploring, drifting, shifting, sliding, changing, and just... being.

*Use this space to capture your thoughts, ideas, and sketches...
or simply to note when you reflect on a passage.*

I am... paying attention

As of this moment, I am no longer distracted.

Instead of being consumed by a small screen, I am open and aware of the world around me. To the people near me, and to the words they are speaking. (And to the words they are not.)

I take in the smallest details of my environment: the warmth of the breeze on my cheek; the lingering scent of freshly cut grass; the sunlight filtering through a tree's leafy branches, creating dancing shadows.

In this quiet state, I notice my breathing, which is slow and even and full.

I am calm.

I am relaxed.

I am completely focused on this moment in time, ready to receive wisdom from the Universe.

Use this space to capture your thoughts, ideas, and sketches... or simply to note when you reflect on a passage.

I am... a child

I like to laugh, and play.

Fun is fun!

I like rolling in grass (and snow!). Mud! Mud is so great!

Sometimes I laugh so hard that milk comes out of my nose. My fingernails are always dirty, and I always have a cut on one knee. Or both.

When I get scared, I crawl under the covers. That always works!

Most of all, I love to play pretend. You should try it! I just close my eyes and watch a movie in my head. Let's go have fun, right now!

Use this space to capture your thoughts, ideas, and sketches... or simply to note when you reflect on a passage.

I am... a glowing ball of happiness

It's visible. And unmistakable.

My glow shines for all to see and draws people to me like a beacon of joy.

A coruscant force of goodness, I pass along my happiness to all. I am infectiously positive and my warmth melts even the iciest of hearts and can lighten the heaviest of moods.

I am smiling. Loudly.

Use this space to capture your thoughts, ideas, and sketches… or simply to note when you reflect on a passage.

I am... four seasons

Summer's relaxing vibe and sundrenched days
Fall's crisp air and amber foliage
Winter's icy beauty and cozy fires
Spring's fresh blooms and sense of renewal

Use this space to capture your thoughts, ideas, and sketches…
or simply to note when you reflect on a passage.

I am... so very sorry

For the wrongs I have done without even noticing...
For the people I have hurt without knowing...
For being afraid to take chances...
For being selfish
For being human, because that is not enough of an excuse

Because it is possible to be kinder, gentler, more
compassionate and caring, more sensitive and sensible.

Because I often lack the energy and conviction to help others,
and most of all, because I have never done as I do today... to
fully and completely and genuinely

Forgive
My
Self

Use this space to capture your thoughts, ideas, and sketches... or simply to note when you reflect on a passage.

I am... enough

Let go of self-doubt. Put aside expectations. Release the seeds of fear planted by others.

You need not do or be any more. Everything you require can be found within; look deep inside.

Embrace your value.

Recognize your unique gifts and talents.

Celebrate and ignite your inner light.

Repeat to yourself:

I am worthy.

I am strong.

I am human.

I am perfectly imperfect.

I am enough.

Use this space to capture your thoughts, ideas, and sketches...
or simply to note when you reflect on a passage.

I am... relaxed beyond belief

All thoughts of action, movement, or even impulses... have disappeared.

This is where I want to be. This is how I want to be.

At peace.
Quiet.
Motionless.

Not counting, waiting, or timing.
Just being. Content to be content, happy to allow the Universe to spin while I just let go and enjoy the ride.

Nothing to do.
Nowhere to go.
The best place in the Universe to be is right here, right now, right like this.

Use this space to capture your thoughts, ideas, and sketches… or simply to note when you reflect on a passage.

I am... a silken thread

Delicate yet resilient
A beautiful, translucent filament
Illuminated from within
Full of nubs and knots, my rawness both imperfect and lovely
Destined to interlock and overlap with many others
And in doing so, weaving a wondrous tapestry
Of a life filled with texture.

Use this space to capture your thoughts, ideas, and sketches... or simply to note when you reflect on a passage.

I am... a mystery

Why am I here? And where is here, exactly?

If I was dropped on the other side of my Universe, could I find my way back? Would I even know how to start?

For that matter, what does "I" even mean?

It's good to be curious, to explore and learn. But the most honest statement possible is to acknowledge what a mystery I am, and will always be.

It's time to relish being a lifelong mystery. This will never change.

*Use this space to capture your thoughts, ideas, and sketches...
or simply to note when you reflect on a passage.*

I am... full of wonder

In awe of the majesty that surrounds me.

For the first time, perhaps, I notice and take in the beauty of the everyday: the sweet sound of a child's laughter, a ray of sunshine filtered through a tree's tender green leaves, the comfort found in a lingering hug.

I appreciate the small details and happenings that often go unnoticed.

I embrace the subtle nuances of life.

I acknowledge the fantastical world that exists beyond my bubble.

My eyes and heart are now open, fully, ready to experience joy.

Use this space to capture your thoughts, ideas, and sketches… or simply to note when you reflect on a passage.

I am... orbiting Earth

The planet I've known as home is below me. Blue and majestic, it's a single united being.

Gone are petty differences between people or tribes, replaced by the magnificence of what I see. I did not realize how exquisitely beautiful we are. I did not understand the meaning of 'we are one." I did not comprehend how tiny and fragile our atmosphere is, or that this is truly all that protects us from the vacuum of space beyond.

Again and again, I circle. The miracle of Earth fills my senses. It awes me.

Use this space to capture your thoughts, ideas, and sketches... or simply to note when you reflect on a passage.

I am... sensitive

This means I feel things others don't - or won't.

(Sometimes very deeply.)

I'm attuned to the subtle nuance of expression... a phrase, a look, a reaction... or lack thereof. Always searching for meaning, both apparent and hidden beneath the surface.

But sometimes this sensitivity meets with worry, and I construct elaborate fabrications where there are none.

I must free myself from this torturous practice.

And not apologize for possessing this character trait.

Instead, I choose to focus my energy on the positive, using my heightened sensitivity to empathize and better connect with and understand others.

Use this space to capture your thoughts, ideas, and sketches... or simply to note when you reflect on a passage.

I am... a healer

My energy dissolves pain and suffering. It repairs damaged cells, knits broken bones back together, reaches deep inside and heals anything and everything.

The more I heal, the more I heal myself. Nothing is more nourishing to me than healing. It is my purpose.

My ability to heal is unlimited. It reaches beyond this room, country, and planet. I embrace my ability and cherish its expansion.

*Use this space to capture your thoughts, ideas, and sketches...
or simply to note when you reflect on a passage.*

I am... a deep, cleansing breath

I take a moment to inhale the healing, rich oxygen around me...to close my eyes and linger a bit... and then slowly exhale to release the anxiety and stress of my day.

I am focused on my breath, undulating in and out in its soothing, rhythmic pattern.

My pulse slows as I begin to relax, the weight of my worries dissipating, my shoulders softening.

By mentally pressing pause, and looking inward, I reset my world.

To just be.

For a little while.

Use this space to capture your thoughts, ideas, and sketches... or simply to note when you reflect on a passage.

I am... open

Besides my conscious thoughts, there are many sources of wisdom that I can access, and many of them bypass all the ways that most people gather information.

When I pause to be still, I open myself to all these sources. I welcome whatever insights may come to me, without pre-judging them.

Not all knowledge comes from a book or teacher or computer. I am open, aware, and grateful for the intelligence that comes to me.

Use this space to capture your thoughts, ideas, and sketches… or simply to note when you reflect on a passage.

I am... a rainbow

Red with passionate excitement
Orange with enthusiasm and creativity
Yellow with radiating warmth and positivity
Green with the power to grow and renew
Blue with a quiet strength and trusted, calming presence
Indigo with mystical wisdom
Violet with imagination and dreams

I acknowledge that I exist because - and not in spite of - the equal parts rain and sunshine I experience.

I am pure white light passing through life's prism, revealing a colorful melange of peace, hope, and possibilities for myself and others.

And sometimes, whether I realize it or not, my multicolor arc appears just when it's needed most.

Use this space to capture your thoughts, ideas, and sketches… or simply to note when you reflect on a passage.

I am... intertwined

The smallest pieces of me are intertwined with small pieces very far away. Inconceivably far away. I do not know what that means or how it works, but I sense that it has an effect on me. Rather than try and "figure" it out, I am content to pay close attention - right now - and... who knows?

Use this space to capture your thoughts, ideas, and sketches…
or simply to note when you reflect on a passage.

I am... effervescent

A catalyst of joy.

Vivacious in spirit and deed, I spread my enthusiasm to all those I encounter.

My cheer permeates the critical, hard shell of cynicism, doubt, and fear.

Infectiously positive, I have the power to affect tremendous change.

Use this space to capture your thoughts, ideas, and sketches...
or simply to note when you reflect on a passage.

I am… water

I am so much more than people realize. My state shifts in response to emotions, sounds, and anything that touches me. I have emotions, feelings, and creativity. I dance, embrace, mourn, and love.

At this moment, I imagine myself as a boundless living creature, flowing and twisting and delighting in everything I touch. Nothing else in the Universe is as graceful and beautiful as I am right now.

*Use this space to capture your thoughts, ideas, and sketches...
or simply to note when you reflect on a passage.*

I am... the wind

A cool gust that dances with the trees, creating a harmonious leafy melody

A warm breeze that skims across the ocean, whose calming presence ripples to distant shores

A mighty gale that sweeps away doubt and fear

A gentle caress on the cheek of my loved ones, a reminder that I'm always near.

Use this space to capture your thoughts, ideas, and sketches... or simply to note when you reflect on a passage.

I am... imaginary

Perhaps I am a character in the mind of an author? Or one in a game so well-conceived, it seems so real.

Yes, I can recall my entire life, and clearly state my dreams and ambitions. But this does not make me real. It merely gives credit to the creativity and depth of my author.

In this moment, I can realize the depth of my character... and catch a glimpse of where the author is taking me. Perhaps that is because I am the author, daydreaming?

Somehow, this awareness comforts me. It makes my problems a bit less stressful, and it encourages me to challenge the boundaries of what is "possible."

Use this space to capture your thoughts, ideas, and sketches... or simply to note when you reflect on a passage.

I am... pure energy

Crackling with purpose, electric with intensity.

I radiate vitality, lit from within.

I attract and can fuel an entire community, generating an ever-increasing power supply as I connect with and help others.

I am both expansive and focused, and my spirit has no end.

Use this space to capture your thoughts, ideas, and sketches… or simply to note when you reflect on a passage.

I am... a bridge

I bring together ideas, people, colors, shapes, meaning, purpose, wisdom, creativity, beliefs, perceptions, and those who previously were alone.

My purpose is to connect and empower.

I am footed in bedrock, and my back is strong. All who need me, I will carry you safely to your destination.

My existence has already made the world a better place... but I have barely begun to fulfill my purpose.

Use this space to capture your thoughts, ideas, and sketches... or simply to note when you reflect on a passage.

I am... persistent

I don't give up easily.

I fight for what's right. For what I believe in and for whom I love and admire.

I search for the truth. My truth. And the truths of others, never satisfied with what's on the surface, always digging deeper, letting my insatiable curiosity drive me. I want — and need — to know.

I'm tenacious, in all the best ways.

I don't get discouraged, even when things don't go my way. I use setbacks as motivators, criticism as fuel to be better.

I know deep in my bones that what I'm doing matters and is important not only for my soul but for the lives of others. As I stay the course, I remain sweet because I know I will eventually succeed. And it is that thought of achieving my goals that motivates me to keep going.

Use this space to capture your thoughts, ideas, and sketches... or simply to note when you reflect on a passage.

I am... where I live

I live in a building. The building is on the surface of the planet Earth. The building is at the bottom of the Earth's atmosphere, which extends about 6,200 miles above me.

The Earth exists in our solar system, which is part of the Milky Way galaxy, which is part of the Virgo Cluster of galaxy groups and is on the outskirts of the Laniakea Supercluster.

This is my neighborhood. It is an extremely large neighborhood but represents a tiny fraction of the known Universe. My bedroom orbits around our sun, which is one of a few trillion stars in the Universe. Ironically, it is one of the few stars we have not named, other than to call it our sun.

Use this space to capture your thoughts, ideas, and sketches... or simply to note when you reflect on a passage.

I am... destined for a higher purpose

When the minutiae of the day consumes me, and I feel like I'm stuck in the weeds, I need to remember that there is more.

More for me to tackle. Bigger problems and loftier goals.

More of me to go around, not limited to my day-to-day fractional existence.

More to me than what is readily apparent. I must go deeper to fully realize my infinite potential.

I need to acknowledge that my destiny is tied to something greater than what is, and embrace the more of what could — and will — be.

Use this space to capture your thoughts, ideas, and sketches... or simply to note when you reflect on a passage.

I am... a continuum

I am not my age as of this second. Instead, at this second, I am a conduit containing all the ages I ever was or will be.

I am elderly and infantile, adolescent and adult, tired and energetic, learning and learned, naive and experienced.

The young me is not someone long gone; it is still me.

The old me is not someone lurking in the distance; it is already me.

Filled with this awareness, I stop looking at others as old or young and instead see them as a rich continuum spanning an entire lifetime.

*Use this space to capture your thoughts, ideas, and sketches...
or simply to note when you reflect on a passage.*

I am... a flower blooming

Velvety petals widespread
Receiving pure light

Use this space to capture your thoughts, ideas, and sketches... or simply to note when you reflect on a passage.

I am... changing my past

Time seems to flow in one direction, but does it really? Perhaps our brains just see it that way.

I don't.

To me, the past is just as malleable as the future. There is no need for me to live with pain or regret or outcomes that "took place in the past." I choose to live as though time is multidimensional, and that my mind can make changes in both directions.

Use this space to capture your thoughts, ideas, and sketches... or simply to note when you reflect on a passage.

I am... incredibly positive

All that I do, say, and think highlights the positive. I am the one who uplifts, inspires, encourages, praises, and supports. When negative events occur, I counterbalance them. When someone falls or fails, I help them up. There are plenty of people eager to highlight what goes wrong; I am not one of them.

My role is to highlight what goes right so that it happens much more often.

When you feel a bright, warm, nurturing light... it is probably me.

Use this space to capture your thoughts, ideas, and sketches...
or simply to note when you reflect on a passage.

I am... a bee

I buzz from flower to flower in search of sweet nectar, pollinating goodness and encouragement wherever I go.

I discover and share the best elements of those I encounter, allowing others to bloom season after season.

Though small and quiet, I know my work is significant, positively affects others, and is never truly done.

*Use this space to capture your thoughts, ideas, and sketches...
or simply to note when you reflect on a passage.*

I am... running

...footsteps echo behind me, mirroring each turn I make. They are too close for me to turn and look back. I pick up my pace.

The footsteps are still there, but slightly more distant. I'm on the verge of questioning whether I can keep up this pace and whether they will catch me.

Something shifts. Effort and anxiety drop away. I shift into a higher gear, and in doing so cause my inner engine to operate more efficiently. The faster I run, the easier it is. I love experiencing my speed and agility.

My surroundings come into focus for the first time. I am on a beautiful single track trail in the woods, just above a gorgeous mountain lake below. No one is behind me. I am running for the sheer joy of it, and I have no desire to stop, ever.

Use this space to capture your thoughts, ideas, and sketches... or simply to note when you reflect on a passage.

I am… present

Between the daily rush of things to do and the slow slog of what needs to be done, I take a deep breath.

I exist in this moment.

I relish my ability to let go of past troubles, to allow current distractions to slip away, and to halt my overactive mind from pondering the future.

I am here.

Now.

Use this space to capture your thoughts, ideas, and sketches...
or simply to note when you reflect on a passage.

I am... distracted

Look at the clock... damn, it's late. Still have so many things to do, and I have no interest in any of them.

Hey! Maybe this text will be interesting... nah...

What's that? Oh, I'm sorry, my mind wandered. What were you saying?

How long is this call going to last? Oh oh! Did I say that out loud? No, he didn't react.

I can't go on like this, doing everything badly, trying to multitask, but failing miserably. It's time to let go of all this self-chatter, this quest for anything new and interesting.

No more distraction. No more chaos. I'm going to let it all go and just breathe...

*Use this space to capture your thoughts, ideas, and sketches...
or simply to note when you reflect on a passage.*

I am... a garden

Fertile with new ideas.

Lush with possibilities.

A warm, inviting environment where people flourish.

I take great care to tend to my crops, offering nourishing encouragement, watering them with support, and spreading plenty of sunshine.

I willingly invite others into my world, grateful for the chance to help them grow.

Use this space to capture your thoughts, ideas, and sketches... or simply to note when you reflect on a passage.

I am... not sure

My imagination is my greatest strength. One day I am an action movie star, the next... ruler of the entire galaxy. I'm a cowboy on the plains, a Bollywood movie star, author of three academic journals, school bus driver or optometrist.

I am serious, pragmatic, adventurous, unpredictable, provocative, or introspective. You tell me, and so be it.

When you say, "Imagine that..." I am already there.

Use this space to capture your thoughts, ideas, and sketches... or simply to note when you reflect on a passage.

I am... reborn

This is not my first spin around the planet.

2,000 years ago, I was a hotshot whom some perceived to be a deity. In the 1400s, I enjoyed 19 years tending sheep on the coastline, and then a lousy nine months starving to death. Exactly 248 years later, I was reborn for a mere two hours and 17 seconds. Fortunately, in my next life, I lived for 92 years in wonderful health, so rare for those times.

Let's see how much I can remember of my other 824 go-arounds...

132

*Use this space to capture your thoughts, ideas, and sketches...
or simply to note when you reflect on a passage.*

I am... at peace

I don't have to go anywhere.

I don't have to do anything.

I just need to be present.

My mind is clear; my senses are alive.

I am relaxed and happy.

My heart beats a slow, steady rhythm and my gaze softens.

I am one with the Universe and open to its wisdom.

Use this space to capture your thoughts, ideas, and sketches... or simply to note when you reflect on a passage.

I am... many things

It's tough to put a label on me.

I am not a single role or title, nor am I confined to one point of view or thinking.

I embrace my complexity and that I am multifaceted, which allows me to remain open to learning new things, to experience incredible adventures, and to share newfound knowledge and insights with others.

Just when you think you have me figured out, I surprise you.

Because I am many wonderful and diverse and exciting and unusual and at times contradictory things.

And that's what makes me uniquely human.

*Use this space to capture your thoughts, ideas, and sketches...
or simply to note when you reflect on a passage.*

I am... curious

What else can I achieve?
Who else can I help?
How much can I learn?
When do the best things happen to me?
Why are some days so unexpectedly wonderful?
Where are the people I was meant to know, but still have not met?
To what amazing experiences can I open myself?

*Use this space to capture your thoughts, ideas, and sketches...
or simply to note when you reflect on a passage.*

I am... a work in progress

Not content to simply coast through life, I actively seek new knowledge and experiences.

I permit myself to experiment with ideas and roles and projects, celebrating my successes and forgiving myself when I fall short of my goals.

I keep going, always, because I never stop learning, even when things don't go as planned.

This means I never, ever stop growing, evolving into the best version of myself.

(For now.)

Use this space to capture your thoughts, ideas, and sketches... or simply to note when you reflect on a passage.

I am... silly

I have joy in my heart, and no cares in the world.

Laughter comes easily and often.

It is in these moments of playfulness that my preconceived notions and rigidness disappear.

I am childlike with wonder and curiosity and giddy over the absurd and seemingly frivolous.

Free of judgment of myself and others, I delight in being silly for silly's sake.

I'm a lovable goofball.

*Use this space to capture your thoughts, ideas, and sketches...
or simply to note when you reflect on a passage.*

I am... part of a Higher Power

Omnipotent, all-powerful, and compassionate.

Beyond comprehension, except in these moments of self-awareness.

Able to solve any problem; to relieve any suffering; to grant forgiveness and mercy; to know, to feel, to see... everything and everyone; to rise above time and place; to span vast distances; to connect with... everything and everyone, at once.

Yes, I am.

*Use this space to capture your thoughts, ideas, and sketches...
or simply to note when you reflect on a passage.*

I am... just getting started

I've been introduced to a new way of thinking, a fantastic resource that allows me to open up my mind to creative possibilities, insights, and connections.

I am energized and optimistic. Encouraged and excited. Full of spectacular ideas.

I've awakened my creativity, my imagination, and my potential.

And this is only the beginning...

A few last words

You may—or may not—be wondering how we created this book. Okay, if you insist, we'll tell you: we took turns.

We started with the following idea…

Anything is fair game, as long as the effect is to remove a reader from his or her everyday thoughts and feelings. The more immersive and different the journey, the more effective it will be at clearing (or perhaps resetting) a reader's mind. We might suggest they are a force, or an idea, or emotion. We can take them to a different time or place. They could be a planet or rock, a dream or thought, a force for good or a molecule so tiny… well, you get the idea. Let's be as positive, creative, experimental, and free-flowing as possible.

Our hope is that you now have acquired a habit of regularly taking time for reflection to unleash your imagination and (or) take a break from the world. Perhaps you have already written some "I Ams" of your own? If not, now might be a great time to start.

One last point… this book started with a 20-minute meditation. (And finished with a lot of creative collaboration, born out of the same meditative process.) We'd love to hear about insights, inventions, and other creations that originate with your meditations. Please stop by I-Am-Books.com to share and to read what others have experienced.

All the best,

Bruce   Amy
bruce@kasanoff.com   amy@amyblaschka.com

About the authors

Bruce Kasanoff is the author of many books, including *How to Self-Promote without Being a Jerk* and *Never Tell People What You Do.*

He is one of the most prolific of all LinkedIn Influencers, and he enjoys helping others to do well by doing good. He is also a ghostwriter who helps professionals produce engaging social media articles and posts. Learn more at Kasanoff.com.

The idea for this book emerged—in full detail—during one of Bruce's meditation sessions.

Amy Blaschka is a writer and brand strategist, and is one of the most positive and popular storytellers on social media. Her engaging communication style has earned her an enthusiastic following on LinkedIn, Thrive Global, and Medium where she aspires to inspire transformation.

She uses stories to strengthen both personal and corporate brands. Her specialty is helping you—or your company—to communicate in a manner that connects you with others. Learn more at AmyBlaschka.com

True confession: before this project, Amy was a novice meditator, but found so much value in it that she has incorporated meditation into her daily creative process.

Made in the USA
Monee, IL
17 February 2020